# HOKA-HEY = COMPLETENESS

SELECTED HAIKU

HOKA-HEY = COMPLETENESS: SELECTED HAIKU

by Stefanie Bennett



This publication is made possible by a gift and grant from - THE GOLDEN HILL INDIAN NATION at Trumbull, Connecticut, USA and in agreement with the author in 2019.

HOKA-HEY = COMPLETENESS: SELECTED HAIKU is a combined Cochon & Golden Hill publication



ISBN 978 1 877010 93 4

Published by
Burringbah Books
PO Box 368
North Hobart
Tasmania 7002

Dedicated to Wilma & Harold Piper - Vicki Curro Piper & Minnie Ellis Piper Zanesfield, Ohio (plus) Aurelius Piper Snr. & family, Trumbull, Connecticut.

# HOKA-HEY = COMPLETENESS

SELECTED HAIKU

by

STEFANIE BENNETT

During 'Diamonds & Rust'

Joan Baez

# CONTENTS

ITALO CALVINO / EPIGRAM / ONE-NESS

CLIMATE EMERGENCY / RE-READING 1984 / THE PACIFIST

INDIGO YEARS / OVER IT / REBELLION

TROUGH / PRETENDING TO BE ME / HUMAN AFFAIRS

COMMUNE / EVOLUTION / STONEHENGE

DEVINE VISION / AKHMATOVA 'LIGHTS OUT' /
    DEMOGRAPHICS

REVELATION / FATE / PRECISION

THE POCKET DESKTOP / SUBTITLES / REALM

PROJECT / TRANSMISSION / ANT RID

CROWING / SCORE / TIME TRAVELLER

BEDAZZLED / TRANSLATION / EARTH WATCH

LATE EDITION / CLASSICISM / QUEST

THE FOX / HAZE / HOKA-HEY = COMPLETENESS

REFLECTION / SKILL / BOUNTY

TIDE / OBSERVATION / CULTURE

COUNTING COUP = FRACKING / THE BACK
    COUNTRY / TEA FOR TWO

REVIVAL / VISUALLY ACTIVE / OBSERVATORY

BEWITCHED / DOWNLOAD / METEOR PROGNOSIS

NUCLEAR SCIENCE / REFERENCE / MULTI-TASKING

OSCAR WILDE / NIGHTFALL KARMA / SORROW

REPOSE / LANTERN PARADE / EGOCIDE

CALENDAR / LOG BOOK / HEAVEN'S GATE

FIRST EDITION / DINNER GUEST / GENGHIS KHAN

GINSBERG: HOWL / SPLASH / DIAGRAM

## ACKNOWLEDGEMENTS

Some of these poems have been published in…
Poems From The Paddy Wagon, The Medium, Shade, One Plus Two, The North Brisbane College of Advanced Education, Dead Snakes, Shot Glass Journal, Cosh, UFO Gigolo, Tomato Press, Khasmik Poets, Stanzaic Stylings, Whispers, Standing Rock, Kind of A Hurricane Press, High Coupe, Record Magazine, Poetry Super Highway, Haiku Universe, The Australian, World Haiku Series 2019, Akita International Haiku Network, others…


**Cover Photo**: Tania Kavney
**Rear Photo**: Stefanie Bennett - and the poem SEQUENCE


Once again, a very large thank you to those who have supported my work of words over the last few years. I thank you for the time you have given me. Also, in 2007 the coming together of Australian groups ie; the ACF, CFA, Arts Action For Peace and others joined the call for a 'nuclear free world.' ICAN - The International Campaign to Abolish Nuclear Weapons was born. I am proud and indebted to my lot for having won the 2017 Nobel Peace Prize.

## ABOUT THE AUTHOR

Stefanie Bennett has published over a dozen volumes of poetry, a libretto and a novel. She has tutored in The Institute of Modern Languages (James Cook University), acted as a published editor…and worked with [No Nukes] Arts Action For Peace. Of mixed heritage (Irish/Italian/Paugussett-Shawnee) she was born in QLD. Australia in 1945. Stefanie, an ex-blues singer and musician has been fluent internationally in poetry online and in print journals. She has been nominated for Best of the Net and The Pushcart.

## TIME-LINE QUOTES

Beyond Bennett's undoubted technical skills, however, is the quality which elevates her to the top rank of Australian poets. (Tim Thorne)

If we frame her as a surrealist following poets like Eluard and Aragon, we are able to view those symbols as expressions of some notion of true life. (Simon Eales)

Stefanie Bennett — I believe the poetry content matter is rattling magnificent. (Poetry Pacific: Zem Karlos)

After 'Wen & The Red Candle'. This superb poem is not only beautifully written, but also all the more remarkable for capturing a very Asian poetic voice despite being written in a distinctly 'western' style. (Robert Lavett Smith)

… Of all the women poets she has the greatest range and her writing is interesting even when it's pretentious. (Frank Kellaway)

There are pieces of real excellence, a call, at once witty and emotional for enduring, intelligent sisterhood. (Cheryl Frost)

No-one knew for sure where you were really at… now onward for your love of all the poets. (Robert Adamson)

To whom shall I go to learn about the one I love?

Kabir says: "When you are trying
to find a hardwood forest
it seems wise to know
what a tree is."


[1440-1518]

## SPEAK

Holding one's tongue:

the weight

of it


## TICK-TOCK

Reading about sea-slugs

they crept up

on me


## DAY DREAM

Just a conga-line

of forthright

sheep

## NO ROARING TWENTIES

… The Bodhi tree's

wind chime

& rain patter


## CROSS CURRENTS

Now you hear it

then you don't:

grass chatter


## FAULT LINE

The feisty fire-ant plays

scrabble

on the gravel

## COLLECTIVE MEMORY

When the phone rings

I know

it's hell calling

## TENDRILS

Electioneering…

it's raining

fiction

## FOG BOUND

Getting over myself:

violets

into dust

# FUSION

Bell-bottom trousers

hanging

in the mist


# SUMMIT

A chorus of blackbirds:

the eye

of the sky


# CAUGHT

The outrider

pinching

the punch

# ASCETICS

Get rid of the evidence!

There's no such thing

as a monkey mask…


# CARBON COPY

Seen on the lip of 'time':

the embattled

rose-bud


# THE CRIMEA

Bogus-like swords

cross

at the junction

# MOON LANDING 2

You can't have the world

and eat it

too

# ALCHEMY

The East wind must be

the West wind

blown round

# POST MODERNISM

My conversation with

a chrysalis

I will not tell

# THE SWALLOW

Pecking Buddha's

pocket:

"water music"


# THE POSTMAN

Storm cloud calligraphy

reads like

a sutra


# TALLY

Earth's inheritance

those

not listening

# BELLINGEN ISLAND

The flying-fox flits past

Gaea's

moon face

# (DEAR) PRUDENCE

It's never known

who

we run into

# FOOTPRINTS

The crimson rosella:

bringing

the inside out

## CASH & CARRY

It's what didn't get said

that matters

most


## WORRY-BEADS

The bucket-list

went

walk-about


## TEMPLE

Atop the ant hill

the purple

iris

## GOD'S DESIGN

All mosquitoes are

the amorous

kind


## THE GREY

Tethered to the barber-pole

a long-haired

retriever


## TRILOGY

Re-fried beans…

rattles

the salt shaker

## ILLUMINATION

A bemused dragonfly

studying

the bee's knees


## GREGORIAN CALENDAR

Cry freedom: there's one

flaming star

down


## THE HURT

Another overcast day

without regret

or ritual

## OLD WARRIOR ASKS...

Tree stump:

> how do

> you do?


## VICTORY

The ivory carnation

> black-belts

> the lawn mower


## "HOWZAT" (how's that)

A lizard playing

> 'dodgem'

> on the pitch

## COLD WAR 2

The lone geranium

in the field

of fury


## INSIGHT

Unattended note-book:

correcting

the rhyme & spine


## OTHERNESS

Raindrops on the roof:

spirit

drumming

# MASTERPIECE

That back-yard

water dragon

winks laterally


# SURROUND SOUND

Claw deep in cloud

the red-winged

hawk


# SITCOM

Klaxton horn

afraid of

itself

## BLUE MOON

In the water:

a face frowns

upside down


## EXCHANGE

Tipping the busker:

sad eyes

raining


## SPRING

Letting her hair down!

the top-knot

pigeon

## EVOLUTION

First past the post:

a riderless

horse

## COMMENTARY

Osaka typhoon: the books

do not

balance

## EQUATIONS

Afternoon tea:

the tarmac's

no fly-by

# REFUGE

What kind of animal would I be

if I wasn't

an animal


# SWAT TEAM

Falling asleep:

the day's

reckoning


# A SOMBRERO TERCET

Headless mannequins

all

in a row

# WEATHER-COCK WARNING

Erratic chimes!

clock down!

lock down!


# 'AHA'

Waves reign and wave in

the barking

breakers


# CHUCKLE

Poems brushed swiftly flow

into the world's

back-pack

## IDYLL

A Boobook owl joins

the chorus

of September rain


## TWO LEGGED WORLD

Friends attained:

a game

of hide-and-seek


## UNBALANCED

It's raining

cats & rats

on Wall St.

## TRICKSTER

Left behind:

the midnight train to

Sydney


## OCEANIA

Nothing to disclose

but the stone jaw

of Rapanui


## THE 7th WONDER

A pilgrim without

progress

on stilts

## HUNGER

A shrunken earth's Eden:

why?

ask the asp


## AMBIENCE

One handed — the cobbler

picks up his trade

& walks off


## HOG-TIE

A thinking-cap

gets

no credit

## COSMIC SHOWER

It's just Chief Joseph

taking care

of business


## MOON 'SUITE'

Lemon-lime and bitters

and a little

solstice on rye


## ASTRAY

Mind in a muddle:

thoughts

unheard of

## EACH SEASON

Speaking your name
I rearrange
the photo-frame


## BREXIT

… The war
of
The Shrubs!


## PRIMAEVAL SHIFT

Beside a sea-wall's
harbour lights
2 meer-cats kissing

## AURORA BOREALIS [R.I.P.]

Long time gone

house

of song


## THE CLASSICS

Gentile centipede

romancing

the stone


## FOOL PROOF

The half-moon and I

share

the same rocker

## ITALO CALVINO

Baking beans:
nothing left
to hunt


## EPIGRAM

Yeti's paw-print:
the orb
of the sun


## ONE-NESS

The sound of goodbye
laid to waste
the ebb-tide

# CLIMATE EMERGENCY

Once we were young...

too old for

the killing fields


# RE-READING 1984

Dante's

cart-wheeling....

derby


# THE PACIFIST

Call 'the sandman'

a raindrop's

crashed

## INDIGO YEARS

A snap dragon's

tough

weed-hood


## OVER IT

Mail stamped to self:

'return

to sender'


## REBELLION

The hazy sun fell off

God's cat-daddy

wagon

## TROUGH

Let's call a truce:

  the old woman

    & the sea


## PRETENDING TO BE ME

A blithe spirit:

  the bearded

   stranger


## HUMAN AFFAIRS

Sin city…

   apple

 turn-over

## COMMUNE

The grass-spear: it's

a wayward ant's

freeway


## EVOLUTION

So lonely talking

into

the cat's ear


## STONEHENGE

What's to come carries

itself

away

# DIVINE VISION

As the kettle whistles

the butter-knife

curtsies


# AKHMATOVA 'LIGHTS OUT'

All those who tampered

long before:

apply within


# DEMOGRAPHICS

Look! the two pine trees

grow nearer

together

## REVELATION

Foretold: the hairbrush

is having

a grey day


## FATE

Waiting on the phone

to pick me

up


## PRECISION

It split the axe handle:

a cracker

of a frost

# THE POCKET DESKTOP

The Book of Change

or failed

revisioning?


## SUBTITLES

Run-away rogue…

attention in

detention


## REALM

Lilacs in the sand:

still-life

hallucinates

## PROJECT

Dog days…

a postman

on the run


## TRANSMISSION

Enlivened neighbours:

doing the karaoke

chicken-walk


## ANT RID

Ribbit! calling on

a citizen's

arrest

## CROWING

Watch your head:

it's what

the sky said


## SCORE

Warring for peace:

like the slug

I'll nap on it


## TIME TRAVELLER

Never having

to say

sorry

## BEDAZZLED

Reflective store-front

mirror:

don't look back


## TRANSLATION

Reading a teacup

the headlines

carry guns


## EARTH WATCH

Midlife:

cobwebs

& clover

## LATE EDITION

In the cupboard the worn

sweat-shirt

of mourning


## CLASSICISM

The coming attraction:

a mosquito

hums Mozart


## QUEST

A hitch-hiking haiku

texts

Kerouac

## THE FOX

Nonchalant chasing

of winter's

passing


## HAZE

The art of forgetting:

not written

yet


## HOKA-HEY = COMPLETENESS

Cushioning the half-moon

the most

distant of lovers

# REFLECTION

No doubt about it:
the sour dough
is on the rise…


# SKILL

A hard-hat quietly
looking for
its head


# BOUNTY

The magenta Buddha
handshakes
the morning glory

## TIDE

At world's end? The words

I would

leave you


## OBSERVATION

An aged mulberry tree

attracts

snakes & ladders


## CULTURE

What a cracked lid:

the coffee

grinder

## COUNTING COUP = FRACKING

The drill-bit

    tortured

    my teeth


## THE BACK COUNTRY

Sunrise seen through

    a bandicoot's

        ears


## TEA FOR TWO

Finger food:

  who eats

    it…

## REVIVAL

High noon: the summit

in my back-

pocket


## VISUALLY ACTIVE

The drone's got

a no-parking

ticket


## OBSERVATORY

A carnival of fireflies

in a lamp-lit

stairwell

# BEWITCHED

The drain-pipe hit

the ground

running

# DOWNLOAD

Arms race! nothing

to do with

heart & head

# METEOR PROGNOSIS

See! Montezuma's at

tomorrow's

hard-rock cafe

## NUCLEAR SCIENCE

An uncivil war…

riches

and lust


## REFERENCE

It's a conundrum: not that

I miss you

but by how much


## MULTI-TASKING

The aged orbit the earth

before

leaving…

## OSCAR WILDE

The poetry of the earth

has no

bar-code


## NIGHTFALL KARMA

The rock said

don't

do it


## SORROW

Why is the black night

painting

the town red…

## REPOSE

A spade is a spade

    that won't come

when you call it


## LANTERN PARADE

Strange bed-fellows

    the harp

    and the king


## EGOCIDE

… Dill pickle

    feeds

the intellect

# CALENDAR

Above the bramble bush

Vincent's

starry night

# LOG BOOK

Love me or leave me:

the grass

continues to grow

# HEAVEN'S GATE

World-speak… what

does she say:

'run…'

## FIRST EDITION

Read my mind…

turning

away


## DINNER GUEST

A fasting

space-

cadet


## GENGHIS KHAN

'A fine catch'

thus spake

my father

## GINSBERG: HOWL

Hush! The ink-well

is throwing

a tantrum


## SPLASH

That corporate mind:

just another fly

in my soup


## DIAGRAM

Remembering your face

in asset rich

firelight

www.ingramcontent.com/pod-product-compliance
Lightning Source LLC
Chambersburg PA
CBHW030651190726
48286CB00008B/2769